I0063227

TEENS SOAR IN THEIR CREDIT SCORE

Cheurlie Pierre-Russell

Publishing Information

Printed in the United States of America. All rights reserved. Except as permitted under the U.S. Copyright Act of 1976, no part of this publication may be reproduced, distributed or transmitted in any form or by any means, or stored in a database or retrieval system, without the prior written permission of the publisher.

This is a work of nonfiction. The information presented within is told with the express permission of the real characters whose names are protected for confidentiality.

Any other resemblance to actual persons, living or dead, business establishments, events or locales is entirely coincidental and incidental to the real events in the time period this information is conveyed is placed.

Copyright © 2020

Cheurlie Pierre-Russell

Miami, Florida

Table of Contents

1. Teens Maturing.. 4

2. Terms to Understand 6

3. No Score to Credit Score 9

4. Protecting Yourself 15

5. Payment History 16

6. Card Cancellation.. 19

7. New Credit Insight 20

8. Student Loans.. 24

9. Collections Account... 28

10. Conclusion 30

BOOKS BY C. PIERRE-RUSSELL

For Younger Readers:

Alani Story ABC Book

Little Kitty Goes to School

Sheila the Shy Shark

A Princess Is Born

Picture Books:

Broken Before the Storm

The Beauty of Love in Those We Shame

The Special Little Sister

Save the Missing Penny

Making Dollars Make Sense: Business Owner at Any Age

Friendly Monsters: Behind the Computer

For Older Readers:

The Better Betty

The Love of Likes

Butter Me Fly: My Way Home

Judge Me Now

Teens Soar in Their Credit Score

1. Teens Maturing

Becoming a teenager is the central turning point in a child's life. Teens go from having no responsibility one day to having tons of responsibilities the next, and without guidance, it's impossible to know how to navigate this transition. One of the biggest new responsibilities every teen faces is developing financial literacy—in other words, learning how to take responsibility for their finances and make good choices. That's why all teenagers need to know how crucial their credit score is and the impact it can have on their future.

In the world of credit, an 800 is a perfect score. This book serves as valuable reference to guide you in getting to that coveted 800 credit score. You will learn how to establish credit in an intelligent way, how to avoid mishaps that damage your credit score, and how to maintain your credit score using proper behavior.

It is very important to learn financial literacy during this stage of life, early on. As a teen, you will be able to start building your credit, which is why learning about credit now will benefit your financial status later in life. Your credit score can be initiated between the ages of thirteen and fifteen years old, and starting now will put you in a great position as you grow older and start to make decisions like applying for student loans, leasing a vehicle, or mortgaging a home.

This book summarizes all the important information you need so you can soar with your credit score and have an advantage that will benefit you throughout your life.

Teenagers are forced to mature to become more personal, integrative, and practical in response to their individual lives and responsibilities. As a teenager, your decisions become more critical as you mature and your thought process begins to shift into post-formal and dialectical thoughts. This book will help you transition your thought process into setting adult formulated goals and take appropriate actions to achieve them. In this way, you will establish your priorities in life.

Setting goals for building your credit score will help you to formulate and implement long-term goals for your life. Although understanding how to build and manage your credit score can be a bit overwhelming for adolescents to learn, this book will help to guide you. Reading this book will equip you with the knowledge and skills you need to learn how to create, build, and manage your credit score. Several examples are provided for clarity to help you understand the credit calculations and relations for the numbers required.

Financial Goals:

_____

_____

_____

_____

_____

2. Terms to Understand

When it comes to understanding your credit score, there are several important credit terms you should know. In this section, we'll teach you those terms and define them for you.

The term **credit bureau** refers to a company that collects information relating to the credit rating of a person and monitors and manages the individual's credit score to make it available to credit card companies, financial institutions, and other creditors. In the United States, the three credit bureaus that manage credit scores are Equifax, Experian, and Transunion. These credit bureaus govern and control the activities within the credit scores. All three credit bureaus manage the credit behavior separately. In addition, they will not merge your creditors, payment history, or credit scores with one another. They work solely based on their own report.

A **credit report** is a detailed breakdown of a person's credit history that is prepared by the credit bureau. A credit report is the sum of the information provided to lenders showing the individual's creditworthiness.

The **credit score** is a number that illustrates someone's creditworthiness, and is determined mathematically using the data within a person's credit file. Companies use credit scores to determine a person's level of creditworthiness, using it to decide whether to offer them any credit and/or at which interest rate to offer it. The credit score can range from as low as 300 points up to 850 points, with anything 800 and above constituting a perfect score. Therefore, the higher your credit score, the more money you save with credit lenders when applying for credit or loans. For example, an individual who has a 750 credit score may get approved for a mortgage at a 2.75 percent interest rate. On the other hand, a person who has a credit score of 580 may be denied a mortgage loan or may get approved for a mortgage loan with a high 5.25 percent interest rate. The lower the credit score, the higher interest rate you will be charged for any credit.

The term **credit utilization** simply means the amount of money you used on the credit card compared to the amount of credit you have been given by the lender. The credit utilization is important because it is worth 30 percent of the credit score.

The **credit usage** is an exact representation of how someone uses their credit and how much creditworthiness they show. It's the amount of money you owe on the credit card comparing to the total available credit limit amount. Credit advisors recommend that a credit usage of less than 30 percent is considered a healthy amount, while other credit experts recommend a credit usage of less than 20 percent is a healthy amount. In line with both the credit advisors and the credit experts, past experience has shown that sticking to 20 to 25 percent of credit usage for each card proves excellent creditworthiness.

The **credit history** is a record showing the borrower's responsibility in repayment of debts.

The credit history is monitored for Equifax and Transunion on www.creditkarma.com for FREE. In addition, your credit history can be obtained directly from the three credit bureaus; they give one free credit report per year. If you would like to order more credit reports from the credit bureaus, you will be charged a fee unless you received a credit denial from a creditor.

The term **payment history** is the record of on-time, late, and missed payments made on past and current credit accounts. The payment history applies to each and every account listed on your credit report. In addition, the payment history comprises 35 percent of the total credit score and is the most important factor affecting credit score calculations. Listed below is the telephone contact information for each of the bureaus:

Credit Bureau	Mailing Address	Phone Number
TransUnion	P.O. Box 1000 Chester, PA 19022	1-800-916-8800
Equifax	P.O. Box 740241 Atlanta, GA 30374-0241	1-800-685-1111
Experian	P.O. Box 2104 Allen, TX 75013-0949	1-888-397-3742

3. No Score to Credit Score

A. Becoming an Authorized User:
You can start to gain credit as early as thirteen years of age for some creditors and fifteen years of age for others. Becoming an authorized user of an existing account is the most convenient, cost-effective, and logical way to build credit. As an authorized user, a trusted adult will add you to their account and you will receive a credit card for that same account. The primary card holder's responsible dedication will help boost your credit.

But a word of warning: This is only a good idea if you and the cardholder both trust each other to use the card and pay the amount incurred responsibly. You'll also want to make sure the card in question reports authorized users to the three major credit bureaus. The best part of being an authorized user is that you receive an automatic approval, avoid any hard inquiries, and opt out from receiving any credit denial.

As a teenager, you absolutely should not keep a copy of the card in hand. You have two options to prove your maturity: cut the card and trash it or give it to the family member/individual who added you to the account to hold for you. Remember, you are still new to understanding how credit works and it can be very easy to be tempted into misusing the person's credit.

The only difficult part of this option is finding a reliable, creditworthy family member/individual who possesses a stable and consistent credit history. The two most important pieces of information regarding someone's credit account you must focus on prior to being added to their credit file are the credit usage and the credit age.

The credit usage on the account should consistently be within the 20–30 percent range noted in the previous section. In time, when you become more experienced and apply for your own card, you will be able to use your 20 percent credit on your credit card. Becoming an authorized user first will train you to keep the same frame of mind and good behavior that you displayed when building your credit. If the card limit is $1,000, you should never spend more than $200 on the card. The leftover $800 in available credit should always be left untouched.

For the credit age, you want to focus on someone with two-plus years of history. The longer the credit age, the better the history of the account for your credit report. This will be a great benefit for the authorized user because when you get added to the account you will receive the same credit age showing as the open date as the individual/family who established the account, giving you years of experience on paper.

Credit Age:

Owner Account	Credit Limit	Opened	Monthly Payment	Open Balance
Yal Showne	1,000	July 7, 2013	$45	$200

Author-ized User	Credit Limit	Opened	Monthly Payment	Open Balance
David Lowe	1,000	July 7, 2013	$45	$200

B. Finding a Trustworthy Cosigner:

As a teenager, finding a trustworthy person whose credit age and credit card usage match what we described above is key to building strong credit. If the individual you are authorized with spends more than 30 percent on their credit card, it can harm your credit score. Remember, your goal is to build your credit score, not damage it prior to receiving a card yourself! You do not want to add your Social Security number to a bad account. Therefore, make sure to find a credible individual who has maintained a great credit history. Once you've verified their trustworthiness, ask that individual to add you to two to three credit accounts to start building your credit.

Verify they are a trustworthy cosigner by reviewing their credit card statements to make sure that they are a good fit for building your credit score. For example, if the family member/individual's credit card limit is $1,000, you want to make sure they didn't charge more than $200 to $300 on that $1,000 credit card limit, which represents 20 to 30 percent of credit usage. Therefore, the available credit should never be less than $700 on that credit card. The chart below shows a usage balance on the account of $200, which proves the credit card has a $800 available credit.

Possible Trust Worthy Cosigners:

_____

_____

Example Credit Usage:

Owner Account	Credit Limit	Opened	Available Credit	Monthly Payment	Usage Balance
Yal Showne	1,000	July 7, 2013	$800	$45	$200

Owner Account	Credit Limit	Opened	Available Credit	Monthly Payment	Usage Balance
David Lowe	1,000	July 7, 2013	$800	$45	$200

Chart – Personal Credit Use:

Company Name	Credit Limit	Safe Usage	Usage Balance	Available Credit

C. Establishing Credit through Employment:
Another alternative option teenagers can use to establish credit is by getting a job. Getting a job will prove some sort income to help you establish credit. The CARD Act of 2009 requires students and other young adults to demonstrate their ability to repay debt before they can open a credit card account. Having a job will help you do exactly that, and it strengthens your qualifications for getting a credit card of your own.

D. Applying for a Secure Credit Card:
Another way you can start to establish credit is through a secure credit card, which you can apply for starting at age eighteen. Secure credit cards are offered by several banks. These are credit cards that are given to you to use your own money as the collateral on the card. Because you are using your own money, it allows you to be vigilant and responsible with the charges that are placed on the credit card. You can start with as little as $300 to $500 on the secure credit card, depending on the bank's decision. The process is fairly simple. You can go to the bank and tell them you are applying for a secure credit card. The bank will process the secure card and asked for the funds to be placed on the card. That secure credit card now becomes a credit card, and the credit is established. The credit usage applies to every credit card. The goal is to spend, on average, about 25 percent of the total credit limit. *For example, if the secured credit card amount totals $500, you can only spend about $125 on the credit card.* Card providers may even raise the credit limit or offer you an unsecured credit card after a period of responsible use.

Understanding the Spending Limit:

Credit Total (x) Credit Usage % (=) Amount ABLE to Spend

Credit Total	Credit Usage	Amount ABLE to Spend
$500	0.25 or 25%	$125

Credit Total (-) Amount ABLE to Spend (=) Amount NEVER to Spend

Credit Total	Credit Usage Amount	Amount NEVER to Spend
$500	$125	$375

Chart Example #1 – Personal Spending Limit Calculation:

Credit Total	Credit Usage	Amount ABLE to Spend

Credit Total	Credit Usage Amount	Amount NEVER to Spend

Chart Example #2 – Personal Spending Limit Calculation:

Credit Total	Credit Usage	Amount ABLE to Spend

Credit Total	Credit Usage Amount	Amount NEVER to Spend

4. Protecting Yourself

As a teenager, you must understand that your Social Security identification number is a very serious matter. Your Social Security number serves as your permanent identity in many different situations throughout your life. Applying for a job, school, a bank account, or college are all situations where you will be required to add your Social Security number on the business document. Therefore, you need to remember your Social Security number and use it for business purposes only. Your Social Security number should never be emailed, left on a voicemail, exposed, transferred via text message, stored in your cell phone, written on a piece of paper, or input in front of others to memorize. You should always safeguard your Social Security number to protect yourself from becoming a victim of fraud or identity theft.

Your Social Security card should always be left at home. Memorize the number and place the card in a safe location where no one else will be able to access it. If someone gets your Social Security number, they can essentially become you. They may be able to collect tax refunds, collect benefits and income, commit crimes, make purchases, set up phone numbers and websites, establish residences, and use health insurance—all in your name.

5. Payment History

The payment history is crucial to your credit score because a good payment history proves responsibility and trustworthiness. The payment history is a record of your payment behavior on all credit accounts. Payments must always be made on time because this determines whether your credit score will increase or decrease on a monthly basis. In fact, this factor is so important that it accounts for 35 percent of the overall credit score! The data listed below contains information about one credit account that is in good standing.

Payment History
You've made **100%** of payments for this account on time.

	J	F	M	A	M	J	J	A	S	O	N	D
2020	√	√	√	√								
2019	√	√	√	√	√	√	√	√	√	√	√	√
2018	√	√	√	√	√	√	√	√	√	√	√	√
2017								√	√	√	√	√
2016												
2015												
2014												

Last payment   Apr. 01, 2020

Current Payment Status   Current

Amount Past Due $0

Worst Payment Status   Current

Minimum Monthly Payment $25

Opened   May 31, 2013 (6 yrs, 10 mos)

Account Details

Account Status	OPEN
Type	Credit Card
Responsibility	Authorized User
Remarks	No Info
Times 30/60/90 Days Late	0/0/0
Closed	No Info

The payment history above is an example of a payment history on a credit report. The chart shows all the detailed information for this particular credit account, which was established on May 31, 2013. The account history shows the card has been open for 6 years and 10 months. The individual on this account is an authorized user of this account. The minimum monthly payment for this account is $25 and this account holder has never missed a payment. **Was this authorized user added to a suitable credit account? (Hint: Focus on credit age and payment history.)**

Credit card payments should be made at least *five days prior to statement date.* Previous experience shows that processing your credit card payments five days prior to the payment date will help prevent you from missing your monthly payments due to processing time delays. If your payments are mailed off early, they will always be received on time. Similarly, your online payments and automatic payments should always be processed five days prior to the credit card statement date.

Another tip to boost your credit score is to *pay extra on your monthly bill.* Instead of paying your monthly statement amount you should add half of the payment as an additional amount on top of the monthly payment. This process proves you are creditable. If you are able to pay the balance of the credit card off every month after use, it proves you are a winner. To build good credit and stay out of debt, you should always aim to pay off your credit card bill in full every month. Paying it off in full helps eliminate added interest and shows you are trustworthy. In addition, paying your credit card off helps reduce your credit utilization and thereby increases your credit score.

If you forget to make your payment on the statement date, you should send the payment off immediately. Paying the credit card balance after the statement date can result in a hefty late fee and a possible increase in interest rate. Paying your credit card late can have a negative effect on your credit score, too. When the late payment is made, you can write a letter to the creditor asking them to remove the late payment from your account. It is called a *good faith letter* because you are asking the creditor for a favor. It is up to the creditor to honor your written request and remove the late payment information from your credit report. Late payments can hurt your payment history by decreasing your credit score and putting you in a higher risk bracket. Paying your bills on time builds a positive payment history on your credit report and could increase your chances of getting credit when you need it.

6. Card Cancellation

Avoid canceling a credit card if you have a balance on the account as it can hurt your credit score tremendously. Depending on your total available credit, closing a credit card account with a high credit limit could harm your credit score, particularly if you have high balances on other cards or loans. If you have a zero balance and your credit utilization rate is zero you will not be impacted by the loss of a balance. You can simply stop using the card. It's good practice to avoid cancelling a credit card, as it can do more harm to your credit than good on your credit report.

7. New Credit Insight

As a teenager, you may be oblivious to understanding how hard inquiries can affect the credit score. The first step a bank takes when you apply for a new credit card or loan is to pull your credit report. There are two types of inquiries the lender uses to make a credit decision: a hard inquiry or a soft inquiry.

The hard inquiries happen when a lender or credit card issuer looks at your credit to make a lending decision. This can lower your credit score. The more hard inquiries pulled, the more points will be deducted from your credit score. Hard inquiries from things like credit applications can stay on your report for up to two years, but their effects tend to fade over time.

On the other hand, soft inquiries typically occur when a person or company checks your credit as part of a background check. This kind of inquiry won't affect your credit score. A hard inquiry will negatively impact your credit factor on your credit score. But if you only have one or two credit inquiries on your report within the last twelve months, the impact will be minimal.

Below are two different scenarios to show what a credit file looks like in the inquiry detail section of the credit report. The first example shows that this individual had "no hard inquiries" found on the credit report. The second example shows there was a hard inquiry pulled on this credit report. The inquiry gives the date it was pulled, the company's name and contact information, and the date it will be deleted off the report.

Example #1: No Hard Inquiries

Clean slate! As of Apr. 13, 2020, you have no inquiries on your credit report.

Example #2: Hard Inquiry Listed

Credco
Inquiry from Mar 25, 2020   - Finance

This inquiry could stay on your report until Apr. 2022.

See an error?
Find out how to dispute a hard inquiry

Institution Information
Credco
SAN DIEGO, CA
92150
(800) 523-0233

Teenagers quickly realize you are being introduced to and offered credit everywhere you go. For instance, as you walk around the mall, every store you enter will try to offer you a 10 or 15 percent discount if you apply for a new credit card. Avoid being swindled in applying for credit to receive the discount on your purchase. Creditors have a way of persuading adolescents into applying for credit cards to receive a discount during their purchase, but their main goal is to promote their business, gain a profit, and increase their sell. Every business's goal is to convert that 10 or 15 percent discount into a large profit gain of hundreds of dollars. The company's profit gain comes from the high interest rate offered to you on the store credit card. Although the creditor offered you a discount in the front end when you made your purchase, they will recoup that money and more on the back end of the credit card agreement.

For example, imagine that a $300 credit card with a 24 percent annual rate is given to you at a clothing store. The store clerk will inform you of a 15 percent discount on all of your purchases made that particular day when you use the new credit card. If your purchase price totals $150 and you were given the 15 percent discount on your purchase, you will be charged $127.50 on the new credit card.

The annual percentage rate (APR) is the rate you're charged over twelve months, which comes out to 2 percent per month. Since months vary in length, credit cards break down APR even further into a daily periodic rate (DPR). It's the APR divided by 365, which would be 0.065 percent per day for a card with a 24 percent APR.

Example:

$150 total X 15% discount = $22.50 (amount saved on purchase)

$150 - $22.50 = $127.50 (purchase charge on credit card)

$127.50 X 24% APR = $30.60 (interest hold for the year)

$30.60 / 12 MONTHS = $2.55 (monthly interest rate)

Therefore, if you do not pay the $127.50 in full the following month with the $2.55 annual percentage rate, which will total $130.05, you will find yourself paying

$158.10 in twelve months as each portion of the monthly payments will have an interest of $2.55. Or, if you decide to just pay your minimum monthly payments as calculated over a two-year period, you will owe $188.70 = $127.50 + $30.60 (2). Over a two-year period, that 15 percent discount of $22.50 actually cost you $61.20 in interest. That is $61.20 in interest - $22.50 discount amount = $38.70 of decreased, lost, and wasted money.

8. Student Loans

Entering college can feel stressful, exciting, and scary, all at the same time. Keep in mind that college is not designed to pay you as a job; rather, it is designed to teach you. As a post-secondary student, you are gaining more from college by receiving your education than you'd gain from any money earned. You must attend college with the mind frame that receiving your education is beneficial enough to forego financial gain for now.

Many students think they're taking advantage of the situation by applying for excessive student loans, but this decision can be disastrous for your credit score. If a student loan is needed to cover your education, accept the amount to cover your tuition only. Any excess amount should be refunded back to student services. For instance, if your tuition fee is $2,500 but you were approved for a student loan of $4,000 for the semester, accept the funds and return the remaining $1,500 to the disbursement department immediately. This way, you'll minimize your loan balance.

Remember, student loans are granted to cover your tuition cost and other expenses. Those other expenses can be eliminated by making smart decisions. For instance, if you spend a lot of money on food, go to the school's cafeteria where you can eat for free through your financial aid grant.

You must be very diligent when requesting student loan money, as the more money you request, the higher your debt becomes. Federal student loans have no statute of limitations; therefore, they can try to collect student loan debt forever. Although the student loan payments may be deferred for some years, the debt itself being placed on the credit file will affect your credit score. Having a large amount of student loans may have a negative impact on you later in life. Years down the road you may find yourself being rejected when applying for any credit, such as mortgage and car loans.

Student loans affect the credit score by adding all of the loans disbursements to your report. The list of disbursements showing the full amount of the student loan will later increase your debt-to-income (DTI) ratio. Your DTI is all your debts that you are responsible for paying every month compared to the amount of income you receive per month. Having a high debt-to-income ratio proves to the bank that your debts—all of your monthly bills—surpass the amount of income you are receiving. In contrast, a low debt-to-income ratio shows the bank you are responsible.

Student loans should only be taken when absolutely needed. If you can live off of your financial aid grant, avoid student loans altogether. For example, if all of your monthly bills/debt payments, including your student loans but excluding living expenses such as utility bills, food, and entertainment, total up to $1,500 a month and your monthly gross earning is $2,000, you may be denied credit. Your DTI ratio is 75 percent, which proves you are in the red zone. If you have over 50 percent DTI, it proves more than half of your income before taxes is going toward debt payments.

Total monthly debt payments

------------------------------------- X   100 = ___%

    Monthly gross income

Example:

$1500

--------- X 100 = 75% (take action to lower your debt payments)

$2000

Debt-to-Income Ratio Level

0%	35% 49%	100%

0-35% — Looking good

The balance between your income before taxes and your debt is at a manageable level. You most likely have money left over for saving or spending after you've paid your bills. Lenders view a lower DTI as favorable.

36-49% — Opportunity to improve

Your debt is being maintained, but you may want to lower your DTI to put you in a better position to handle unexpected expenses. Lenders may ask for additional eligibility factors.

50–100% — Take action

More than half of your income before taxes is going toward debt payments, which means you may not have much money left to save, spend, or handle unexpected expenses. Lenders may limit your borrowing options.

Chart – Personal DTI Calculation:

_____ X 100 =   %

_____ X 100 =   %

_____ X 100 =   %

_____ X 100 =   %

9. Collections Account

Collections accounts are debts that have gone unpaid. An account goes into collections when you have fallen behind on payments for a certain amount of time. Collections are a continuation of debt owed that will remain on your credit report for up to seven years from the date the debt first became delinquent—or unpaid—and was not brought current. After seven long years, the negative information will automatically be removed from your credit report, even if a collection agency assumes the debt. For those seven years, however, having such a debt on your credit report can make your life very difficult and impact your ability to get a loan, rent an apartment, buy a property, and more.

Example of section on credit report:

Example 1: No Collection Found

> *Clean slate! As of Apr. 13, 2020, you have no collection accounts on your credit report.*

Example 2: Collection Documented— Derogatory Marks

I C System $140

Opened   February   Original creditor: 11 ATT U
12, 2019   VERSE

Overview

You've paid
off **0%** of your col-   Opened   Feb 12, 2019 (1 yr, 2 mos)
lection amount

Balance	Highest Balance	Account status	Open
$140	$140	Type	--
		Responsibility	Individual
		Remarks	Place for collection
		Original Creditor Name	11 ATT U VERSE

10. Conclusion

Your credit score is your ticket to a financially stable future. By building and using your credit score strategically while you're still a teenager, you will have a head start on building up credit and save so much money later in life. If you take anything away from this guide, let it be that the major key to managing an excellent credit score is to save and become monetarily established. You will be able to save a lot of money simply by having a high credit score because you will be offered lower interest rates on things like mortgages, car loans, and credit cards.

The earlier you decide to start building and managing your credit, the sooner you can become a homeowner or an investor. For example, building your credit prior to age 18 and having steady income for two consecutive years will qualify you in the real estate market to become a first-time home buyer by the age of 21. Concentrate on learning and understanding how your credit score works so that you can benefit from your hard work with strong finances later in life. With the help of this guide, you can set yourself apart from the rest. What are you waiting for? It's time to prove to yourself and those around you that you are a winning example of teen who learned how to take control of their credit score and lay a strong foundation for success in their adult life.

www.ingramcontent.com/pod-product-compliance
Lightning Source LLC
Chambersburg PA
CBHW040931210326
41597CB00030B/5261